"Listen and Learn a Language" - German

Written By:

Kim Mitzo Thompson

Karen Mitzo Hilderbrand

Artist:
Goran Kozjak

Graphic Artist:
Steve Ruttner

Twin 411 - **"Listen and Learn a Language"** - German - ISBN # 1-882331-27-3

"Focus Group" of educators, experts, language translation professionals, and language vocal coaches that contributed to "Listen and Learn a Language."

Corporate Language Services
Various Translators

Eric Morgan
German Teacher
Hudson, Ohio

Lea Jane Berinati
Language Vocal Coach

Eric Morgan
Recording Language Coach

Hal Wright
Producer, Arranger, Vocal Coach

Dear Teacher or Parent:

Thank you for purchasing **"Listen and Learn a Language"** - **German**. We are excited to introduce this unique language series designed to encourage learners of all ages to begin to speak a foreign language. Through music, rhythm, and repetition, German words and phrases will be easy to learn and memorize.

Side 1 is primarily for English speaking persons who wish to begin to learn German words and phrases.

Side 2 is primarily for German speaking persons who wish to learn English as a second language. Both sides of the cassette are great for bilingual instruction where students are encouraged to become fluent in German and English.

Twin Sisters Productions wishes to thank our **"Focus Group"** of experts and teachers, as well as our professional translators, who have dedicated their time and talent to help ensure that **"Listen and Learn a Language"** - **German** is an educationally sound language program.

Sincerely,

Kim Mitzo Thompson
Karen Mitzo Hilderbrand
Twin Sisters Productions, Inc.

Please note: The song lyrics have been translated literally to ensure similiar meanings in both languages.

Table of Contents

Side 1 - English to German

Seite 2 - Deutsche ins Englisch

Supplemental Materials/ Zusatzmaterial

The Alphabet Song

Can you say the alphabet in German? It's easy if you say the alphabet in rhythm. Listen to me.

A B C D E F G
H I J K
L M N O P
Q R S T U V
W X Y Z

The Alphabet is easy to learn
Speak in rhythm
Each letter gets a turn

It's your turn now, repeat after me:

A B C D E F G
H I J K
L M N O P
Q R S T U V
W X Y Z

A B C D E F G
H I J K
L M N O P
Q R S T U V
W X Y Z

The Alphabet is easy to learn
Speak in rhythm
Each letter gets a turn

One more time:

A B C D E F G
H I J K
L M N O P
Q R S T U V
W X Y Z

A B C D E F G
H I J K
L M N O P
Q R S T U V
W X Y Z

NOTE: The letters A, O, and U can have umlauts (two dots) over them which change the way the vowels are pronounced. Example: Ä, Ö, and Ü.

Numbers to Twenty

Jumping rope to a counting song.
Count with me and jump along.
Let's count to the number 10.
Then up to 20 and we'll start again.

Jumping rope to a counting song.
Count with me and jump along.
Up to the number twenty we'll go.
And all the numbers soon you'll know!

one	eins	eleven	elf
two	zwei	twelve	zwölf
three	drei	thirteen	dreizehn
four	vier	fourteen	vierzehn
five	fünf	fifteen	fünfzehn
six	sechs	sixteen	sechzehn
seven	sieben	seventeen	siebzehn
eight	acht	eighteen	achtzehn
nine	neun	nineteen	neunzehn
ten	zehn	twenty	zwanzig

Jumping rope to a counting song.
I'm tired of counting and jumping along.
We know our numbers each and every one.
Counting to twenty was lots of fun!

Learning Colors

We are going to teach you how to pronounce each color name.
Listen carefully and soon you will know all of the colors. Are you ready?

red	rot		rot	red
blue	blau		blau	blue
green	grün		grün	green
yellow	gelb	Great. Now let's say each color in German and then in English.	gelb	yellow
orange	orange		orange	orange
purple	violett		violett	purple
pink	rosa		rosa	pink
brown	braun		braun	brown
black	schwarz		schwarz	black
white	weiß		weiß	white

grün
green

rot
red

braun
brown

rosa
pink

blau
blue

violett
purple

gelb
yellow

weiß
white

orange
orange

schwarz
black

NOTE: The symbol "ß" is the same as the double s (ss) sound in English.

The Days of The Week

You can learn the days of the week if you listen carefully.
Sonntag, Montag, Dienstag, Mittwoch, Donnerstag, Freitag, Samstag

Sunday	**Sonntag**
Monday	**Montag**
Tuesday	**Dienstag**
Wednesday	**Mittwoch**
Thursday	**Donnerstag**
Friday	**Freitag**
Saturday	**Samstag**

Jetzt lernen wir die Wochentage. Hör gut zu.
Sunday, Monday, Tuesday, Wednesday, Thursday, Friday, Saturday.

Sunday	**Sonntag**
Monday	**Montag**
Tuesday	**Dienstag**
Wednesday	**Mittwoch**
Thursday	**Donnerstag**
Friday	**Freitag**
Saturday	**Samstag**

We've just learned the days of the week. Next time won't you sing with me?
Jetzt haben wir die Wochentage schon gelernt. Sing doch mal mit!

SUNDAY	MONDAY	TUESDAY	WEDNESDAY	THURSDAY	FRIDAY	SATURDAY
1 Sonntag	2 Montag	3 Dienstag	4 Mittwoch	5 Donnerstag	6 Freitag	7 Samstag
8	9	10	11	12	13	14
15	16	17	18	19	20	21
22	23	24	25	26	27	28
29	30	31				

Name The Animals

Can you name the animals?
Can you say their names?
Can you name the animals
in this animal naming game?

There's an elephant (Elefant),
a lion (Löwe),
a seal (Seehund)
and a bear (Bär).

I see a monkey (Affen),
a giraffe (Giraffe),
a tiger (Tiger)
and a snake (Schlange).

The hippos are sleeping.
Die Nilpferde schlafen.

The kangaroos are hopping.
Die Känguruhs hüpfen.

The birds are singing.
Die Vögel singen.

And the zebras don't make a sound.
Und die Zebras sagen nichts.

The Hello Song

Chorus I:
Hello, hello, hello to you
I wish to say, I wish to say, hello to you.
Hallo, hallo, hallo Freunde,
Ich will euch sagen, ich will euch sagen, hallo Freunde.

Chorus II:
Hallo, hallo, hallo Freunde,
Ich will euch sagen, ich will euch sagen, hallo Freunde.
Hello, hello, hello to you
I wish to say, I wish to say, hello to you.

Hello. How are you?
Hallo, wie geht's?
I am good.
Gut, danke.

Hallo, wie geht's?
Hello. How are you?
Es geht.
I am so so.

Repeat Chorus II

What is your name?
Wie heißt du?
My name is Petra.
Ich heiße Petra.

Wie heißt du?
What is your name?
Ich heiße Stefan.
My name is Stefan.

Repeat Chorus

Are you in school?
Gehst du in die Schule?
Yes, I am in school.
Ja, ich gehe in die Schule.

Was lernst du?
What are you learning?
Ich lerne Fremdsprachen.
I am learning different languages.

Repeat Chorus II

It was nice to speak with you.
Es war nett, mit dir zu sprechen.
Goodbye Petra, see you tomorrow.
Auf Wiedersehen, Petra, bis morgen.

Es war nett, mit dir zu sprechen.
It was nice to speak with you.
Auf Wiedersehen, Stefan, bis bald.
Goodbye Stefan, see you later.

Goodbye, goodbye, goodbye to you.
I wish to say, I wish to say, goodbye to you.
Auf Wiedersehen, auf wiedersehen, auf wiedersehen, Freunde.
Ich will euch sagen, ich will euch sagen, auf Wiedersehen.

Let's Eat!

We're sitting around waiting to eat.
Grab your fork, come on --Let's Eat!
Wir sitzen am Tisch, das Essen steht bereit.
Hier ist die Gabel, also - Mahlzeit!

We're sitting around waiting to eat.
Grab your fork, come on --Let's Eat!
Wir sitzen am Tisch, das Essen steht bereit.
Hier ist die Gabel, also - Mahlzeit!

Please pass the.... Bitte, reich mir.......

chicken	**das Hühnchen**
potatoes	**die Kartoffeln**
carrots	**die Möhren**
bread	**das Brot**
meat	**das Fleisch**
corn	**den Mais**
rice	**den Reis**
salad	**den Salat**

We're sitting around waiting to eat.
Grab your fork, come on --Let's Eat!
Wir sitzen am Tisch, das Essen steht bereit.
Hier ist die Gabel, also - Mahlzeit!

Please pass the... Bitte, reich mir.......

fish	**den Fisch**
beans	**die Bohnen**
apples	**die Äpfel**
milk	**die Milch**
peas	**die Erbsen**
bananas	**die Bananen**
pie	**den Kuchen**
cake	**die Torte**

My Family Is Special

My family is special.
Meine Familie ist besonderes.
Let's learn how to say their names.
Wir wollen ihren Namen lernen.

We call them....   Wir nennen sie....

We call them	Wir nennen sie
Mother	**Mutter**
Father	**Vater**
Sister	**Schwester**
Brother	**Bruder**
Grandma	**Oma**
Grandpa	**Opa**
Aunt	**Tante**
Uncle	**Onkel**

die Mutter   der Vater   die Schwester   der Bruder   die Oma   der Opa

"My Family Is Special"

My family is special.
Meine Familie ist besonderes.
We work and play together.
Wir arbeiten und spielen zusammen.
And have fun.
Und haben viel Spaß.
My family is special.
Meine Familie ist besonderes.
Laughing and learning
Lachen und lernen.
Growing together.
Zusammen wachsen.
We're a team.
Wir sind ein Team.

We call them...
Sie heißen.....

Mother	**Mutter**
Father	**Vater**
Sister	**Schwester**
Brother	**Bruder**
Grandma	**Oma**
Grandpa	**Opa**
Aunt	**Tante**
Uncle	**Onkel**

*Repeat Chorus with
German
words first*

 Twin 411 - German

Five Day Weather Forecast

What is the weather like today?
Wie ist heute das Wetter?
It is sunny.
Es ist sonnig.

What is the weather like today?
Wie ist heute das Wetter?
It is cloudy.
Es ist wolkig.

What is the weather like today?
Wie ist heute das Wetter?
It is raining.
Es regnet.

What is the weather like today?
Wie ist heute das Wetter?
It is snowing.
Es schneit.

What is the weather like today?
Wie ist heute das Wetter?
It is cold.
Es ist kalt.

What is the weather like today?
Wie ist heute das Wetter?
It is hot.
Es ist heiß.

"The Five Day Weather Forecast"

It is sunny out today, out today, out today,
It is sunny out today, (sonnig) means sunny.

It is cloudy out today, out today, out today,
It is cloudy out today, (wolkig) means cloudy.

It is raining out today, out today, out today,
It is raining out today, (regnet) means raining.

It is snowing out today, out today, out today,
It is snowing out today, (schneit) means snowing.

It is cold outside today, outside today, outside today,
It is cold outside today, (kalt) means cold.

It is hot outside today, outside today, outside today,
It is hot out today, (heiß) means hot.

What is the weather like today, like today, like today?
What is the weather like today? I want to play.

Is it sunny? Ist es sonnig?
cloudy? wolkig?
raining? Regnet es?
snowing? Schneit es?
cold? kalt?
hot? heiß?
What is it like today?
Wie ist heute das Wetter?

It is sunny out today, out today, out today,
It is sunny out today. Let's go play!

Das Alphabetlied

Kannst du das englische Alphabet aufsagen? Es geht ganz leicht, wenn du das alphabet im Rhythmus aufsagst. Hör erst einmal zu.

A B C D E F G
H I J K
L M N O P
Q R S T U V
W X Y Z

**Wir fangen mit dem Alphabet an
Jetzt sind die
Buchstaben dran!**

Jetzt bist du dran! Sprich mir nach:

A B C D E F G
H I J K
L M N O P
Q R S T U V
W X Y Z

A B C D E F G
H I J K
L M N O P
Q R S T U V
W X Y Z

**Wir fangen mit dem Alphabet an
Jetzt sind die
Buchstaben dran!**

Noch einmal:
A B C D E F G
H I J K
L M N O P
Q R S T U V
W X Y Z

A B C D E F G
H I J K
L M N O P
Q R S T U V
W X Y Z

Die Zahlen bis zwanzig

Beim Seilspringen singen wir ein Lied.
Zählt mit mir in Reih und Glied.
Wir zählen erst einmal bis Zehn,
Dann bis Zwanzig, und wieder gehen.

eins	one
zwei	two
drei	three
vier	four
fünf	five
sechs	six
sieben	seven
acht	eight
neun	nine
zehn	ten

Beim Seilspringen singen wir ein Lied.
Zählt mit mir in Reih und Glied.
Die Zwanzig haben wir erreicht,
Dann gehen die andern Zahlen leicht.

elf	eleven
zwölf	twelve
dreizehn	thirteen
vierzehn	fourteen
fünfzehn	fifteen
sechzehn	sixteen
siebzehn	seventeen
achtzehn	eighteen
neunzehn	nineteen
zwanzig	twenty

Beim Seilspringen singen wir ein Lied.
Genug gezählt, jetzt sind wir müd.
Wir wissen die Zahlen, das ist ganz Klass'-
Bis zwanzig zählen, macht viel Spaß!

Lernen wir die Farben

Jetzt wollen wir lernen, wie die Farben ausgesprochen werden. Dann singen wir das Farbenlied. Seid ihr bereit?

rot	red	red	rot
blau	blue	blue	blau
grün	green	green	grün
gelb	yellow	yellow	gelb
orange	orange	orange	orange
violett	purple	purple	violett
rosa	pink	pink	rosa
braun	brown	brown	braun
schwarz	black	black	schwarz
weiß	white	white	weiß

Wunderbar! Jetzt sagen wir jede Farbe auf Englisch und dann auf Deutsch.

rot
red

grün
green

schwarz
black

violett
purple

blau
blue

weiß
white

rosa
pink

gelb
yellow

braun
brown

orange
orange

Die Tage der Woche

You can learn the days of the week if you listen carefully.
Sonntag, Montag, Dienstag, Mittwoch, Donnerstag, Freitag, Samstag

Sunday	**Sonntag**
Monday	**Montag**
Tuesday	**Dienstag**
Wednesday	**Mittwoch**
Thursday	**Donnerstag**
Friday	**Freitag**
Saturday	**Samstag**

Jetzt lernen wir die Wochentage. Hör gut zu.
Sunday, Monday, Tuesday, Wednesday, Thursday, Friday, Saturday.

Sunday	**Sonntag**
Monday	**Montag**
Tuesday	**Dienstag**
Wednesday	**Mittwoch**
Thursday	**Donnerstag**
Friday	**Freitag**
Saturday	**Samstag**

We've just learned the days of the week. Next time won't you sing with me?
Jetzt haben wir die Wochentage schon gelernt. Sing doch mal mit!

SUNDAY	MONDAY	TUESDAY	WEDNESDAY	THURSDAY	FRIDAY	SATURDAY
1	2	3	4	5	6	7
Sonntag	Montag	Dienstag	Mittwoch	Donnerstag	Freitag	Samstag
8	9	10	11	12	13	14
15	16	17	18	19	20	21
22	23	24	25	26	27	28
29	30	31				

Nennen wir die Tiere

Can you name the animals?
Can you say their names?
Can you name the animals
in this animal naming game?

There's an elephant (Elefant),
a lion (Löwe),
a seal (Seehund)
and a bear (Bär).

I see a monkey (Affen),
a giraffe (Giraffe),
a tiger (Tiger)
and a snake (Schlange).

The hippos are sleeping.
Die Nilpferde schlafen.

The kangaroos are hopping.
Die Känguruhs hüpfen.

The birds are singing.
Die Vögel singen.

And the zebras don't make a sound.
Und die Zebras sagen nichts.

Das 'Hallo' Lied

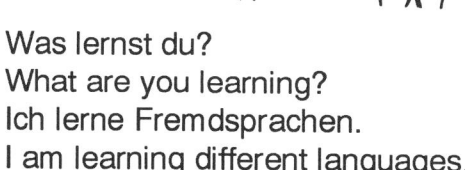

Erster Refrain:
Hello, hello, hello to you
I wish to say, I wish to say, hello to you.
Hallo, hallo, hallo Freunde,
Ich will euch sagen, ich will euch sagen, hallo Freunde.

Zweiter Refrain:
Hallo, hallo, hallo Freunde,
Ich will euch sagen, ich will euch sagen, hallo Freunde.
Hello, hello, hello to you
I wish to say, I wish to say, hello to you.

Hello. How are you?
Hallo, wie geht's?
I am good.
Gut, danke.

Hallo, wie geht's?
Hello. How are you?
Es geht.
I am so so.

Was lernst du?
What are you learning?
Ich lerne Fremdsprachen.
I am learning different languages.

Zweiten Refrain wiederholen

Zweiten Refrain wiederholen

What is your name?
Wie heißt du?
My name is Petra.
Ich heiße Petra.

It was nice to speak with you.
Es war nett, mit dir zu sprechen.
Goodbye Petra, see you tomorrow.
Auf Wiedersehen, Petra, bis morgen.

Wie heißt du?
What is your name?
Ich heiße Stefan.
My name is Stefan.

Es war nett, mit dir zu sprechen.
It was nice to speak with you.
Auf Wiedersehen, Stefan, bis bald.
Goodbye Stefan, see you later.

Ersten Refrain wiederholen

Are you in school?
Gehst du in die Schule?
Yes, I am in school.
Ja, ich gehe in die Schule.

Goodbye, goodbye, goodbye to you.
I wish to say, I wish to say, goodbye to you.
Auf Wiedersehen, auf wiedersehen, auf
wiedersehen, Freunde.
Ich will euch sagen, ich will euch sagen,
auf Wiedersehen.

18

Mahlzeit!

We're sitting around waiting to eat.
Grab your fork, come on --Let's Eat!
Wir sitzen am Tisch, das Essen steht bereit.
Hier ist die Gabel, also - Mahlzeit!

We're sitting around waiting to eat.
Grab your fork, come on --Let's Eat!
Wir sitzen am Tisch, das Essen steht bereit.
Hier ist die Gabel, also - Mahlzeit!

Please pass the.... Bitte, reich mir.......

chicken	**das Hühnchen**
potatoes	**die Kartoffeln**
carrots	**die Möhren**
bread	**das Brot**
meat	**das Fleisch**
corn	**den Mais**
rice	**den Reis**
salad	**den Salat**

We're sitting around waiting to eat.
Grab your fork, come on --Let's Eat!
Wir sitzen am Tisch, das Essen steht bereit.
Hier ist die Gabel, also - Mahlzeit!

Please pass the... Bitte, reich mir.......

fish	**den Fisch**
beans	**die Bohnen**
apples	**die Äpfel**
milk	**die Milch**
peas	**die Erbsen**
bananas	**die Bananen**
pie	**den Kuchen**
cake	**die Torte**

Meine Familie ist besonderes

My family is special.
Meine Familie ist besonderes.
Let's learn how to say their names.
Wir wollen ihren Namen lernen.

We call them....	*Wir nennen sie....*
Mother	**Mutter**
Father	**Vater**
Sister	**Schwester**
Brother	**Bruder**
Grandma	**Oma**
Grandpa	**Opa**
Aunt	**Tante**
Uncle	**Onkel**

Mother	**Father**	**Sister**	**Brother**	**Grandma**	**Grandpa**

"Meine Familie ist besonderes"

My family is special.
Meine Familie ist besonderes.
We work and play together.
Wir arbeiten und spielen zusammen.
And have fun.
Und haben viel Spaß.
My family is special.
Meine Familie ist besonderes.
Laughing and learning
Lachen und lernen.
Growing together.
Zusammen wachsen.
We're a team.
Wir sind ein Team.

We call them...
Sie heißen....

Mother	**Mutter**
Father	**Vater**
Sister	**Schwester**
Brother	**Bruder**
Grandma	**Oma**
Grandpa	**Opa**
Aunt	**Tante**
Uncle	**Onkel**

Wiederhol den Refrain, deutsche Version zuerst.

Der fünf Tage Wetterbericht

What is the weather like today?
Wie ist heute das Wetter?
It is sunny.
Es ist sonnig.

What is the weather like today?
Wie ist heute das Wetter?
It is cloudy.
Es ist wolkig.

What is the weather like today?
Wie ist heute das Wetter?
It is raining.
Es regnet.

What is the weather like today?
Wie ist heute das Wetter?
It is snowing.
Es schneit.

What is the weather like today?
Wie ist heute das Wetter?
It is cold.
Es ist kalt.

What is the weather like today?
Wie ist heute das Wetter?
It is hot.
Es ist heiß.

"Der fünf Tage Wetterbericht"

It is sunny out today, out today, out today,
It is sunny out today, (sonnig) means sunny.

It is cloudy out today, out today, out today,
It is cloudy out today, (wolkig) means cloudy.

It is raining out today, out today, out today,
It is raining out today, (regnet) means raining.

It is snowing out today, out today, out today,
It is snowing out today, (schneit) means snowing.

It is cold outside today, outside today, outside today,
It is cold outside today, (kalt) means cold.

It is hot outside today, outside today, outside today,
It is hot out today, (heiß) means hot.

What is the weather like today, like today, like today?
What is the weather like today? I want to play.

Is it sunny? Ist es sonnig?
cloudy? wolkig?
raining? Regnet es?
snowing? Schneit es?
cold? kalt?
hot? heiß?
What is it like today?
Wie ist heute das Wetter?

It is sunny out today, out today, out today,
It is sunny out today. Let's go play!

Learn 100 words in German/Wir lernen 100 englische Wörter

German Alphabet

A B C D E F
G H I J K
L M N O P
Q R S T U V
W X Y Z

Englisches Alphabet

A B C D E F G
H I J K
L M N O P
Q R S T U V
W X Y Z

Colors/Farben

red	rot
blue	blau
green	grün
yellow	gelb
orange	orange
purple	violett
pink	rosa
brown	braun
black	schwarz
white	weiß

Days of the week/ Wochentage

Sunday	Sonntag
Monday	Montag
Tuesday	Dienstag
Wednesday	Mittwoch
Thursday	Donnerstag
Friday	Freitag
Saturday	Samstag

Numbers/Zahlen

one	eins
two	zwei
three	drei
four	vier
five	fünf
six	sechs
seven	sieben
eight	acht
nine	neun
ten	zehn
eleven	elf
twelve	zwölf
thirteen	dreizehn
fourteen	vierzehn
fifteen	fünfzehn
sixteen	sechzehn
seventeen	siebzehn
eighteen	achtzehn
nineteen	neunzehn
twenty	zwanzig

Family/Familie

Mother	die Mutter
Father	der Vater
Sister	die Schwester
Brother	der Bruder
Grandma	die Oma
Grandpa	der Opa
Aunt	die Tante
Uncle	der Onkel

Learn 100 words in German/Wir lernen 100 englische Wörter

Food/Essen

chicken	das Hühnchen
potatoes	die Kartoffeln
carrots	die Möhren
bread	das Brot
meat	das Fleisch
corn	der Mais
rice	der Reis
salad	der Salat
fish	der Fisch
beans	die Bohnen
apples	die Äpfel
milk	die Milch
peas	die Erbsen
bananas	die Bananen
pie	der Kuchen
cake	die Torte

der Kuchen

Animals/ Tiere

elephant	der Elefant
lion	der Löwe
seal	der Seehund
bear	der Bär
monkey	der Affe
giraffe	die Giraffe
tiger	der Tiger
snake	die Schlange
hippo	das Nilpferd
kangaroo	das Känguruh
bird	der Vogel
zebra	das Zebra

Learn More!/ Lern' mal weiter

fork	Gabel
family	Familie
team	Team
days	Tage
name	Name
school	Schule
special	lieb
tomorrow	morgen
languages	Sprachen
yes	ja
no	nein
German	Deutsch
English	Englisch
to eat	essen
to speak	sprechen
to work	arbeiten
to play	spielen
to laugh	lachen
to learn	lernen
to have fun	Spaß

Weather/ Wetter

sunny	sonnig
cloudy	wolkig
raining	regnet
snowing	schneit
cold	kalt
hot	heiß

Other Twin Sisters Productions' Products

Look for these other available educational audio titles :

EARLY CHILDHOOD and READING READINESS

Phonics 1
Phonics 2
Letters & Numbers
Colors & Shapes
Safe & Sound
Nursery Rhymes
Transportation
Farm Animals
Zoo Animals

Winner of over 20
Major Product
Awards!

FOREIGN LANGUAGE

Spanish
French
German
Italian

MATH

Multiplication
Addition
Subtraction
Division

SOCIAL STUDIES

States & Capitals

SCIENCE

I'd Like To Be An Astronaut
I'd Like To Be A Paleontologist
I'd Like To Be An Entomologist
I'd Like To Be A Marine Biologist
I'd Like To Be A Chemist
I'd Like To Be A Zoologist
I'd Like To Be A Meteorologist
I'd Like To Be A Physicist